TABLE OF CONTENTS

History
- Questions 1
- Answers 15

Memorable Games
- Questions 25
- Answers 35

At the Plate and on the Bases
- Questions 43
- Answers 55

The Battery
- Questions 63
- Answers 75

Photographs
- Questions 83
- Answers 115

Infield
- Questions 119
- Answers 127

Outfield
- Questions 133
- Answers 139

Managers and Coaches
- Questions 143
- Answers 147

Miscellaneous
- Questions 151
- Answers 161

HISTORY QUESTIONS

1. Where was the first Red Sox spring training site?

2. What was the result of Fenway's 1961 All Star Game?

3. What railroad ran between the Huntington Avenue Grounds and the Boston NL field?

4. What ex-Sox members played in four decades?

5. Whom did the Red Sox sign as free agent pitchers during the 1977-78 winter?

6. The Red Sox played an exhibition with what team in Fenway's first baseball action (April, 1912)?

7. Name four all-time greats whose rookie year was 1925 and who spent part of their careers with the Red Sox.

8. Who got the only hit in Bill Rohr's one-hit debut?

History—Questions

9. Name the California Angels pitcher who beaned Tony Conigliaro in August, 1967.

10. Name the New England product touted as the "New Yaz" upon his arrival in 1968.

11. How did the Red Sox acquire Ken Harrelson in 1967?

12. Before Pawtucket became the Red Sox' top farm club in 1973, where was the Sox' AAA team located?

13. Who replaced Sox star Ted Williams when he rejoined the service in the Korean War?

14. How did the then Americans fare in their first opener (April 26, 1901)?

15. Who was the Red Sox' opponent in Fenway's first American League action?

16. Name the Red Sox player whose homer gave the Red Sox a 9-8 1967 victory in a game they once trailed 8-0.

17. What year was the "modern" Fenway Park completed?

18. Whom did Ted Williams homer off of in the 1946 All Star Game?

19. Ned Martin joined the Red Sox as a broadcaster in 1961. Who were his two partners?

20. Of the All-Time Baseball Team members

History—Questions

selected by the Baseball Writer's Association of America in 1969, how many were Red Sox?

21. What is the largest crowd the Red Sox have played in front of?

22. In what year did the Red Sox set their night-game home attendance record?

23. When did the Red Sox set their day-game attendance record of 36,350?

24. What was the added significance of the Red Sox' all-time single-game attendance record day, August 12, 1934?

25. The Red Sox were last world champions in what year?

26. What was the attendance for Ted Williams's historic last game?

27. What park did the Red Sox help open on April 18, 1923?

28. From 1901 to 1907 Boston's American League entry played under several nicknames. What were they?

29. Who did the Red Sox beat in the American League's first extra-inning game?

30. What was Joe McCarthy's controversial pinch-hitting move in the deciding final game of the 1949 season against the Yankees?

31. Who registered the victory for the Tigers

History—Questions

in the decisive game between the Tigers and the Red Sox of the 1972 season?

32. Who joined the Red Sox broadcast team in 1973?

33. When did Ned Martin join the Red Sox broadcast team?

34. Why was a 1939 Sox-Yankees game at Fenway forfeited to the New Yorkers?

35. Whose triples decided Game 5 of the 1912 World Series?

36. Who tripled and then scored while catcher Art Wilson challenged Buck Herzog to tie the later-suspended second game of the 1912 World Series?

37. Whom did the Red Sox receive in exchange for Billy Klaus?

38. Whom did the Red Sox give up for Mike Easler?

39. In 1962 the Red Sox received pitcher Jack Lamabe and first baseman Dick Stuart from the Pittsburgh Pirates in exchange for what two players?

40. Whom did the Red Sox acquire from the Milwaukee Brewers in exchange for Cecil Cooper in 1976?

41. The Red Sox traded Bill Werber to the Philadelphia A's in 1936 for what player?

42. What was the longest game played by the Boston AL franchise?

History—Questions

43. In 1970 whom did the Red Sox receive from the California Angels in exchange for outfielder Tony Conigliaro, catcher Gerry Moses and pitcher Ray Jarvis?

44. In 1966 the Red Sox acquired three players from the Kansas City A's in exchange for outfielder Jim Gosger and pitchers Ken Sanders and Guido Grilli. Name the trio.

45. In 1947 the Red Sox acquired shortstop Vern Stephens and pitcher Jack Kramer from the St. Louis Browns in exchange for what seven players and how much cash?

46. In 1921 who did the Red Sox acquire from the Chicago White Sox in exchange for the legendary Harry Hooper?

47. In 1955 the Red Sox dispatched pitchers Dick Brodowski, Truman Clevenger and Al Curtis along with outfielders Neil Chrisley and Karl Olson to the Washington Senators in exchange for what four players?

48. Previous to Dave Righetti's fourth of July, 1983 effort, what opposing pitcher last no-hit the Sox?

49. What scout signed such Sox stars as Yaz, Rico Petrocelli and Chuck Schilling?

50. Name the player from the Red Sox Golden Age teams of 1912-18 to play on four world champions.

History—Questions

51. In what year did the Red Sox set their Opening Day attendance high?

52. Before Winter Haven, what was the Red Sox last Florida spring training site?

53. Name the Sox player who was traded twice to the club in 1960.

54. Whom did the Red Sox receive from the New York Mets in exchange for Pumpsie Green and Tracy Stallard?

55. What Minnesota Twins pitcher was forced to leave the next-to-the-last game of the 1967 season while on the threshold of giving the Twins the pennant?

56. What was the nickname for the 1967 Boston Red Sox?

57. What team did the Red Sox defeat for their last world championship?

58. What four NL clubs did the Red Sox defeat to win world championships during their 1912-18 Golden Age?

59. What two teams finished one game behind the 1967 Red Sox?

60. Who was the only Red Sox player to wear number 13?

61. Who did the Red Sox receive from the California Angels for Rick Burleson and Butch Hobson?

History—Questions

62. Whose sacrifice fly drove in the deciding run in the 1912 World Series?

63. What injury did Ted Williams suffer in the 1950 All Star Game?

64. What team set a record by leaving 20 runners on base in a 9-inning Fenway game?

65. As the Boston Americans in 1906, what record of futility did the local nine set?

66. When did the Red Sox go on their "champagne" losing streak?

67. The controversial trade of Ken "Hawk" Harrelson in 1969 (along with pitchers Dick Ellsworth and Juan Pizarro) brought what players east from the Cleveland Indians?

68. Who pitched the last no-hitter against the Red Sox at Fenway Park?

69. Name the two American League parks the Red Sox opened other than Yankee Stadium.

70. How did the then Boston Americans do in the home opener of Huntington Avenue Grounds in 1901?

71. The 1946 Red Sox opened their season with a 21-3 record, including a 15-game winning streak. Who halted the Sox record run?

72. What was the additional significance of

History—Questions

the completion of the Sox perfect July, 1967 ten-game road trip?

73. In 1909 what Red Sox player sent an open telegram to Sox fans upon his trade to the St. Louis Browns?

74. The Boston home games in the inaugural World Series (1903) were played at the site of what current university?

75. What three veterans did the Red Sox release with shocking impact prior to the 1974 season?

76. The Red Sox 27-3 loss to Cleveland in 1923 acquired a nickname. What was it?

77. Where was the Red Sox' one-and-only New England spring training site?

78. Who hosted the pregame radio show from Fenway Park and Braves Field in the 1940s and 1950s?

79. Which World Series not including the Red Sox was played at Fenway Park?

80. What did Red Sox owner Harry Frazee receive in exchange for Babe Ruth from Yankee owner Jake Ruppert in 1920?

81. When and where did the Boston American League club play their first game as the Red Sox?

82. Why were the 1904 AL champion Bos-

History—Questions

ton Pilgrims denied a chance to become world champions?

83. What years did Fenway Park host the All Star Game?

84. Who was the Red Sox first free agent signing following the first free agent draft in 1976?

85. Whom did the Red Sox acquire from the St. Louis Cardinals in 1973 in exchange for pitchers Lynn McGlothen, John Curtis and Mike Garman?

86. What is the Red Sox record for most regular-season wins?

87. Who put down a perfect sacrifice bunt in the 9th inning of a 1915 World Series game to set up the winning run?

88. What two Oakland A's stars briefly belonged to the Red Sox in 1976?

89. What is the most runs the Red Sox have ever lost by?

90. Who pinch hit for Babe Ruth in his Fenway Park major league pitching debut?

91. Who was the first Red Sox player to homer in his first major league at-bat?

92. Name the St. Louis Browns catcher to homer his first two major league at-bats at Fenway Park in 1951.

93. What Red Sox rookie defeated Red

History—Questions

Ruffing and the Yankees in the 1938 opener?

94. What New York Yankee's bases-loaded 8th-inning double beat the Red Sox in the pennant-clinching last game of the 1949 season?

95. Whom did the Red Sox acquire for Tris Speaker from the Cleveland Indians in 1916?

96. The Red Sox defeated what Hall of Fame pitcher in the final game of the 1912 World Series despite five errors?

97. What Red Sox player made the final out in Allie Reynolds's second 1951 no-hitter?

98. How did the Red Sox fare in Fenway's first American League game?

99. In what year did the Red Sox win the deciding World Series game in extra innings?

100. Name the midget vaudevillian who "played" third base for Cleveland during a 1946 game.

101. Who made the saving catch for the Sox in the fifth game of the 1912 World Series?

102. The Red Sox received pitcher Rick Wise and outfielder Bernie Carbo from the St. Louis Cardinals in 1973 in exchange for what two players?

History—Questions

103. In 1963 what Cleveland Indians outfielder took a home run away from Dick Williams in perhaps Fenway's most spectacular catch?

104. Who did Carl Yastrzemski take a home run away from in the 1969 All Star Game?

105. The Red Sox and Yankees had a 1967 free-for-all that began when Jim Lonborg hit the opposing pitcher. Name this hurler.

106. Who replaced long-time Sox players Bobby Doerr and Dom DiMaggio following their retirements?

107. What all-time record does Ted Williams share with National Leaguer Rogers Hornsby?

108. What three players did the Red Sox send to the Texas Rangers in exchange for pitcher Ferguson Jenkins?

109. In 1922 the Red Sox acquired pitchers Howard Ehmke and Carl Holling along with first baseman Babe Herman from the Detroit Tigers for what two players?

110. Who is the only man in baseball history to face a pitcher three times in the same inning?

111. Who did the Red Sox acquire from the California Angels in exchange for pitcher Don Aase?

History—Questions

112. What was the preseason exhibition series between the Braves and Red Sox called?

113. The Yankees won a 1967 20-inning marathon against the Red Sox on a hit by whom?

114. Ted Williams's historic game-winning home run in the 1941 All Star Game came off what pitcher?

115. What two numbers have the Red Sox retired?

116. Who succeeded Jim Britt as "Voice of the Red Sox"?

117. What Red Sox slugger escaped from a burning hotel room at the Myles Standish Hotel during the 1947 season?

118. Who is the only American Leaguer to win the MVP award with two different AL teams?

119. Who is the only member of the current Red Sox to play in the 1975 World Series?

120. Name the Red Sox pitcher who was stabbed to death at his own farewell party in 1932.

121. Who was the Red Sox first MVP?

122. In 1937 the Red Sox sent the Ferrells (Rick and Wes), along with outfielder Mel Almada, to Washington for what two players?

History—Questions

123. When did the Red Sox begin to wear numbers?

124. The most homers by a Red Sox team (213) occurred in what year?

125. What Red Sox player broke up two Bob Feller no-hit bids?

126. Who was the Red Sox' first black pitcher?

127. What three black players did the Red Sox try out in 1945?

128. What pitcher's contract did the Red Sox purchase from the Atlanta Braves' Richmond AA club in May, 1971?

129. What two Hall of Famers located the site for Boston's first AL home?

130. Who are the only two Red Sox pitchers in World Series history to win three games in one fall classic?

131. What Red Sox player will be forever remembered for his incredible 13 HR, 40 RBI month of July in 1951?

132. In 1933 the Red Sox sent infielder Harold Warstler, pitcher Bob Kline and $125,000 to the Philadelphia A's to acquire what three players?

ANSWERS

1. Charlottesville, Virginia

2. Suspended 1-1 tie

3. New Haven Railroad

4. Mickey Vernon, Ted Williams, Bobo Newsom, Deacon Jim McGuire, Nick Altrock and Jack Quinn

5. Mike Torrez and Dick Drago

6. Harvard University

7. Red Ruffing, Lefty Grove, Joe Cronin and Jimmie Foxx

8. Elston Howard

9. Jack Hamilton

10. Joe Lahoud

11. He signed as a free agent.

12. Louisville, Kentucky

History—Answers

13. Hoot Evers

14. They lost 10-6 to Philadelphia.

15. The New York Yankees on April 20, 1912

16. Jerry Adair—against California

17. 1934

18. Rip Sewell and his "eephus pitch"

19. Curt Gowdy and Art Gleason

20. Two—Babe Ruth (1914-19) and Lefty Grove (1934-41)

21. 81,841 on May 30, 1938—a doubleheader loss to the Yankees at Yankee Stadium

22. June 28, 1949, when 36,228 saw the team lose to the Yankees 5-4

23. August 7, 1956, when they beat the Yankees 1-0 in 11 innings

24. The doubleheader crowd of 41,766 was treated to Babe Ruth's last Boston appearance before retiring.

25. 1918

26. Only 10,454

27. Yankee Stadium—New York won 4-1.

28. Somersets, Puritans, Pilgrims, Plymouth Rocks and Americans

History—Answers

29. Philadelphia 8-6 in 10 innings

30. He batted Tom Wright for Ellis Kinder—then trailing 1-0 in the top of the 8th. The Yankees then got five runs in the bottom of the inning only to see the Sox score three in the 9th.

31. Mickey Lolich

32. Jim Woods

33. 1960

34. Nearing curfew and leading, the Yankees deliberately put themselves out, sparking a near riot. Umpire Cal Hubbard gave the game to the Yanks. He was later overruled but the game was never made up.

35. Harry Hooper and Steve Yerkes

36. Tris Speaker

37. Jim Busby

38. John Tudor—December 6, 1983

39. Pitcher Don Schwall and Catcher Jim Pagliaroni

40. First baseman George Scott and outfielder Bernie Carbo

41. Mike Higgins

42. 24 innings—the then Boston Americans lost to Philadelphia 4-1.

History—Answers

43. Pitcher Ken Tatum, outfielder Jarvis Tatum and infielder Doug Griffin

44. Pitchers John Wyatt and Roland Sheldon and outfielder Jose Tartabull

45. Catchers Roy Partee and Don Palmer; pitchers Jim Wilson, Al Widmar and Joe Ostrowski; infielder Eddie Pellagrini; outfielder Pete Laydon and $310,000

46. First baseman Shano Collins and outfielder Henry Leibold

47. Pitchers Bob Porterfield and John Schmitz, first baseman Mickey Vernon and outfielder Tom Umphlett

48. Tom Phoebus (April 27, 1968, at Baltimore)

49. Frank "Bots" Nekola

50. Harry Hooper

51. April 14, 1969 against Baltimore (35,343)

52. Sarasota (1933-42, 1946-58)

53. Russ Nixon—first traded for Sammy White, then with Carroll Hardy for Marty Keough and Ted Bowsfield

54. Felix Mantilla

55. Jim Kaat

56. The Cardiac Kids

History—Answers

57. The Chicago Cubs

58. 1912—NY Giants (4-3-1); 1915—Philadelphia Phillies (4-1); 1916—Brooklyn Dodgers (4-1); and 1918—the Chicago Cubs (4-2)

59. Minnesota and Detroit

60. Eldon Auker

61. Carney Lansford, Mark Clear and Rick Miller

62. Larry Gardner

63. A broken left elbow catching Ralph Kiner's fly ball

64. The Yankees (September 21, 1956)

65. They lost 20 straight games, including 19 at home!

66. 1946—the Red Sox carried champagne from Washington to Philadelphia and then Detroit and Cleveland before finally clinching the pennant after six straight defeats.

67. Pitchers Sonny Siebert and Vicente Romo and catcher Joe Azcue

68. Jim Bunning in 1958

69. Shibe Park (Philadelphia) 1909, Griffith Stadium (Washington) 1911

70. They defeated Philadelphia 12-4, Cy Young recording the win.

History—Answers

71. Tiny Bonham of the New York Yankees (2-0)

72. They were greeted by 10,000 fans at Logan Airport.

73. Lou Criger

74. Northeastern (Huntington Avenue Grounds)

75. Orlando Cepeda, Luis Aparicio and Bob Bolin

76. The Indian Massacre

77. Tufts University, Medford, Massachusetts (1943)

78. Gerry O'Leary

79. 1914—the "Miracle Braves" played Games 3 and 4 at Fenway while Braves Field was being built.

80. $125,000 plus a $350,000 mortgage on Fenway Park

81. April 14, 1908, at Washington

82. The New York Giants (NL champions) refused to play a World Series.

83. 1946 and 1961

84. Pitcher Bill Campbell

85. Pitchers Reggie Cleveland and Diego Segui and infielder Terry Hughes

History—Answers

86. 105 (1912)

87. Everett Scott who had two strikes on him

88. Rollie Fingers and Joe Rudi

89. 24—they lost to Cleveland 27-3 on July 7, 1923.

90. Duffy Lewis

91. Pitcher Lefty LeFebvre—off Monty Stratton

92. Bob Nieman

93. Jim Bagby, Jr.

94. Jerry Coleman

95. Pitcher Sam Jones, infielder Fred Thomas and $50,000

96. Christy Matthewson

97. Ted Williams fouled to Yogi Berra twice in a row—the first time Yogi dropped the ball.

98. The Red Sox beat the Yankees 7-6 in 11 innings on April 20, 1912.

99. In 1912 when they beat the New York Giants at Fenway Park with two runs in the last of the 10th

100. Marco Songini—it occurred while Lou Boudreau had his shift on for Ted Williams.

History—Answers

101. Harry Hooper

102. Outfielder Reggie Smith and pitcher Ken Tatum

103. Al Luplow

104. Johnny Bench

105. Thad Tillotson

106. Billy Goodman and Tom Umphlett respectively

107. They are the only two-time "triple crown" winners for their respective leagues.

108. Pitchers Steve Barr and Craig Skok, and outfielder Juan Beniquez—November 17, 1975

109. Second baseman Derill Pratt and pitcher Rip Collins

110. Ted Williams

111. Second baseman Jerry Remy (December 8, 1977)

112. The City Series

113. Horace Clarke

114. Claude Passeau

115. #4 (Joe Cronin) and #9 (Ted Williams)

116. Curt Gowdy

History—Answers

117. Rudy York

118. Jimmie Foxx—Red Sox (1938) and Athletics (1932-33)

119. Dwight Evans

120. Ed Morris

121. Jimmie Foxx (1938)

122. Outfielder Ben Chapman and pitcher Bobo Newsom

123. 1931

124. 1977

125. Bobby Doerr (only hit in each game)

126. Earl Wilson

127. Jackie Robinson, Sam Jethroe and Marvin Williams—none was signed

128. Luis Tiant

129. Hughie Duffy and Tommy McCarthy

130. Bill Dineen (1903) and Joe Wood (1912)

131. Clyde Vollmer

132. Pitchers Lefty Grove and Rube Walberg, and second baseman Max Bishop

MEMORABLE GAMES QUESTIONS

1946 World Series

1. Who led the Sox in batting in the 1946 fall classic?

2. Can you name the Sox' Game 1 starting lineup?

3. Whom did the Cardinals sweep in a two-game NL playoff?

4. Who were the rival managers in the Series?

5. Of the Cardinal regulars, which one led the club in World Series batting?

6. Other than Tom McBride in Games 1 and 2, what other two players made starts in right field?

7. Who won Game 1 for the Red Sox in relief?

8. What currently popular broadcaster appeared in five of the seven games for the Cardinals?

Memorable Games—Questions

9. Who hurled a shutout for the Sox in Game 3?

10. Who pitched the Sox to a 3-2 Series lead in Game 5?

11. Who led the Red Sox with two Series home runs?

12. Name the Red Sox starting catcher in Games 5 and 6.

13. Where was the deciding seventh game played?

14. Who was the Red Sox starter in Game 7?

15. Whose double tied Game 7 at 3-3 in the 8th inning?

16. What Cardinal scored the series-deciding run on Harry "The Hat" Walker's two-out hit-and-run single?

17. Who was the Red Sox' centerfielder?

18. Who was the forever second-guessed cutoff man who hesitated a split-second before making his relay to the plate?

19. Who made the final out for the Sox with two on and two out?

20. Who was the Game 7 loser in relief?

21. Who won three games for the St. Louis Cardinals?

Memorable Games—Questions

October 4, 1948
"The American League's First Playoff"

22. Who was manager Joe McCarthy's surprise Sox starter?

23. What story by Boston sportswriter Dave Egan did the move trigger?

24. Who was the Cleveland offensive star?

25. Name the Indians' 28-year-old rookie lefty knuckleballer who pitched a five-hitter for the win.

26. What Indians player's 4th-inning three-run homer put the game away?

27. Name the Red Sox player who hit a two-run 6th-inning homer to try to get the Sox back in the game.

28. Why was this loss especially bitter for Boston baseball fans?

October 1, 1967
"The Impossible Dream Comes True"

29. Who did the Red Sox defeat on the final day of the 1967 season?

30. What did Yaz do in the finale?

31. Who was the Minnesota starter?

32. What two Red Sox players' errors resulted in a 2-0 Minnesota lead through 5½ innings?

Memorable Games—Questions

33. Who led off the Sox clinching five-run 6th-inning rally with a bunt single?

34. Who followed with singles to load the bases?

35. After Yaz singled to tie the game, whose chopper to shortstop Zolio Versailles tied the game?

36. Who relieved Dean Chance and promptly threw two wild pitches to increase the Sox lead to 5-2?

37. Who made the game's final out?

38. Who defeated the Detroit Tigers in the second game of a Tiger Stadium doubleheader to **finally** give the Red Sox the pennant?

1967 World Series

39. Who was the Red Sox' starter and loser in Games 1 and 4?

40. Can you name the Sox' Game 1 starting lineup?

41. Who led the Cardinals in hitting during the Series?

42. Behind Yaz, what two Sox blasted two Series' home runs each?

43. Who accounted for the Red Sox only run off of Bob Gibson in the Series opener?

Memorable Games—Questions

44. Who got the only Cardinal hit in Jim Lonborg's Game 2 one-hitter?

45. Who was the Red Sox Game 3 starter?

46. Other than the great Bob Gibson with three victories, who was the other Cardinal to post a Series win?

47. The Red Sox tied a World Series record when what three players homered in the 4th inning of Game 6?

48. Who was the Sox Game 6 winner in relief?

49. Name the Cardinal whose three-run homer into the Fenway screen broke open the deciding seventh game?

50. Name the Red Sox pitcher who at 19 years old became the youngest ever to pitch in a World Series?

51. Who led the Sox in hitting during the Series?

1975 World Series

52. Who led the Sox to a Game 1 victory with a five-hit shutout?

53. Can you name the Sox opening game lineup?

54. Who were the Red Sox' '75 playoff victims?

55. Name the Reds' pitcher who won Games 2 and 3 in relief?

Memorable Games—Questions

56. Who doubled in the winning run off Dick Drago in the 9th inning of Game 2?

57. The interference controversy of Game 3 involved what reserve Cincinnati outfielder?

58. Who was the umpire involved in Game 3's dispute?

59. What three Sox homered in Game 3?

60. A gutty complete-game victory in Game 4 by whom tied the series at 2-2?

61. Name the Red Sox player whose two-run triple keyed a five-run 4th-inning in Game 4.

62. Name the Reds slugger who accounted for two homers and four RBI's to lead the Reds to a Game 5 victory?

63. Who was the Series' leading hitter?

64. Who was the only Red Sox starter to be charged with a Series loss?

65. Who were the Game 7 starters?

66. What pitch did Tony Perez hit for his Game 7 homer?

67. What controversial pinch-hitting decision did manager Darrell Johnson make?

68. Who singled to drive in the game-winning runs in both Games 3 and 7?

Memorable Games—Questions

69. Who gave up the Reds' winning hit?

70. Who made the final outs of the 1967 and 1975 World Series and the 1978 AL East Playoff?

October 21-22, 1985
The Sixth Game
"The Greatest Series Game Ever"

71. Who were the starting pitchers in Game 6?

72. A 5th-inning collision left the Fenway crowd in an eerie moment of silence. Who was the Sox player involved?

73. Whose 8th-inning pinch-hit three-run homer tied Game 6?

74. Name the Reds pitcher who allowed the homer.

75. Who scored ahead of Carbo?

76. Who hit the other three-run homer for the Red Sox?

77. Who misinterpreted third base coach Don Zimmer's cry of "no, no, no" as "go, go, go" and was thus thrown out at home in the 9th trying to tag up from third?

78. Dwight Evans's 11th-inning catch, ranking with the greatest in Series history, robbed what Red of a home run?

79. Whom did Carlton Fisk hit his 12th-inning game-winning homer off of?

Memorable Games—Questions

80. What time was Fisk's epochal homer recorded at?

81. What did organist John Kiley immediately break into?

82. Who was the eventual winning pitcher?

83. The Reds tied a Series record with how many pitchers appearing in Game 6?

October 2, 1978
"The Playoff"

84. How did the Red Sox create the playoff?

85. Who were the game's opposing pitchers?

86. Who put the Sox ahead with a 2nd-inning solo homer?

87. Who combined in the 6th to extend Boston's lead to 2-0?

88. Who was aboard for Bucky Dent's infamous two-out three-run 7th-inning homer?

89. What was the count to Dent?

90. Who was Don Zimmer's hapless 7th-inning pinch hitter for Jack Brohamer?

91. What Yankee's homer accounted for the eventual winning run?

92. Who allowed the 8th-inning homer?

93. Who figured in the Red Sox 8th-inning comeback rally?

Memorable Games—Questions

94. In the fateful 9th, a Rick Burleson walk was followed by a Jerry Remy single and a Jim Rice fly to deep center, setting the stage for what final confrontation?

95. What was the result?

96. Name the Yankee not noted for his defensive prowess who made the two key fielding plays of the game.

ANSWERS

1946 World Series

1. Bobby Doerr, 1986 Hall of Fame inductee, with a .409 average

2. 1. McBride rf
   2. Pesky ss
   3. DiMaggio cf
   4. Williams lf
   5. York 1b
   6. Doerr 2b
   7. Higgins 3b
   8. Wagner c
   9. Hughson p

3. The Brooklyn Dodgers

4. Joe Cronin (Red Sox) and Eddie Dyer (Cardinals)

5. Harry Walker with a .412 average

6. Wally Moses (Games 3, 4 and 7) and Leon Culberson (Games 5 and 6)

7. Earl Johnson

Memorable Games—Answers

8. Catcher Joe Garagiola—he hit .316.

9. Dave Ferris

10. Joe Dobson—he allowed only three runs and four hits while pitching a complete game.

11. Rudy York—including a 10th-inning game-winner in the opening game off of Howie Pollet

12. Roy Partee

13. Sportman's Park (St. Louis)

14. Dave Ferris

15. Dom DiMaggio

16. Enos Slaughter—all the way from first in dramatic fashion

17. Leon Culberson—he replaced Dom DiMaggio who was injured while doubling in the tying runs in the top of the inning.

18. Johnny Pesky

19. Pinch hitter Tom McBride hit into a force play, Red Schoendienst to Marty Marion

20. Bob Klinger

21. Harry Brecheen—the first lefty to do so. He won Game 7 on one day's rest.

Memorable Games—Answers

October 4, 1948
"The American League's First Playoff"

22. Denny Galehouse

23. One that stated that Boston's four regular starters, Jack Kramer, Joe Dobson, Mel Parnell, and Ellis Kinder, all begged off the starting assignment.

24. Lou Boudreau—the Indians player/manager had four hits including two homers.

25. Gene Bearden—a war hero from the Pacific theater.

26. Ken Keltner

27. Bobby Doerr

28. It ruined Boston's last chance at a "Subway Series."

October 1, 1967
"The Impossible Dream Comes True"

29. The Minnesota Twins (5-3)

30. He went 4 for 4, drove in the tying runs and threw out the Twins' Bob Allison at second to stop the final Minnesota rally in the 8th inning.

31. Dean Chance

32. George Scott and Carl Yastrzemski

33. Jim Lonborg

Memorable Games—Answers

34. Jerry Adair and Dalton Jones

35. Ken Harrelson

36. Al Worthington

37. Twins' pinch hitter Rich Rollins popped to shortstop Rico Petrocelli.

38. The California Angels (8-5)

1967 World Series

39. Jose Santiago

40. 1. Adair 2b
    2. Jones 3b
    3. Yastrzemski lf
    4. Harrelson rf
    5. Scott 1b
    6. Petrocelli ss
    7. Smith cf
    8. Gibson c
    9. Lonborg p

41. Lou Brock with a .414 average—he also stole seven bases.

42. Reggie Smith and Rico Petrocelli

43. Jose Santiago—with a home run.

44. Julian Javier—double with two out in the 8th inning

45. Gary Bell

46. Nelson Briles with his Game 3 complete-game win

Memorable Games—Answers

47. Rico Petrocelli, Carl Yastrzemski and Reggie Smith

48. John Wyatt—he replaced starter Gary Waslewski.

49. Julian Javier—off of a tired Jim Lonborg pitching on only two days rest

50. Ken Brett

51. Carl Yastrzemski with a .400 average, including three homers

1975 World Series

52. Luis Tiant

53. 1. Evans rf
    2. Doyle 2b
    3. Yastrzemski lf
    4. Fisk c
    5. Lynn cf
    6. Petrocelli 3b
    7. Burleson ss
    8. Cooper 1b
    9. Tiant p

54. The three-time defending world champion Oakland A's—a three-game sweep

55. Rawley Eastwick

56. Ken Griffey

57. Ed Armbrister

58. Larry Barnett

Memorable Games—Answers

59. Carlton Fisk, Bernie Carbo and Dwight Evans—his blast sent the game into extra innings.

60. Luis Tiant

61. Dwight Evans

62. Tony Perez

63. Pete Rose, with a .370 average

64. Reggie Cleveland—the other losing pitchers Dick Drago, Jim Willoughby, and Jim Burton all lost in relief.

65. Don Gullett and Bill Lee

66. The "Leephus" or Bill Lee blooper ball

67. He pinch-hit Cecil Cooper for Jim Willoughby in the 8th with the score tied.

68. Joe Morgan

69. Jim Burton

70. Ironically, Carl Yastrzemski

October 21-22, 1975
The Sixth Game

71. Luis Tiant and Gary Nolan

72. Fred Lynn collided with the wall leaping for a ball in center field.

73. Bernie Carbo

Memorable Games—Answers

74. Will McEnaney

75. Fred Lynn and Rico Petrocelli

76. Fred Lynn

77. Denny Doyle—thrown out by George Foster

78. Joe Morgan

79. Pat Darcy

80. 12:38 a.m. on October 22

81. Handel's "Hallelujah Chorus"

82. Rick Wise

83. Eight

October 2, 1978
"The Playoff"

84. By winning their last seven games while the Yankees lost one.

85. Mike Torrez and Ron Guidry

86. Carl Yastrzemski

87. Rick Burleson doubled and Jim Rice singled him home.

88. Roy White and Chris Chambliss had both singled.

89. An agonizing 0-2

Memorable Games—Answers

90. Bob Bailey

91. Reggie Jackson's drive to the center field bleachers

92. Bob Stanley

93. Jerry Remy doubled and scored on a Yaz single, followed by Fisk and Lynn base hits

94. The Yankees' Rich Gossage against the Red Sox' captain Carl Yastrzemski

95. The star-crossed Yaz popped a 1-0 pitch to Graig Nettles at third and the divisional crown belonged to the Yankees.

96. Lou Piniella—against Fred Lynn in the 6th and against Jerry Remy in the 9th

AT THE PLATE AND ON THE BASES

QUESTIONS

1. This former Red Sox player hit 66 home runs while playing minor league ball in Lincoln, Nebraska. Name the slugger.

2. What league leadership category (for at least one season) do Red Sox players Babe Ruth, Jimmie Foxx, Norm Zauchin, George Scott, Jim Rice and Butch Hobson share?

3. The only pre-WWII member of the 30/30 club—homers and stolen bases—finished his career with the 1929 Red Sox. Name this player.

4. Name the Red Sox player who led the league in stolen bases with 15, the lowest total to lead ever.

5. Who holds the Red Sox record for most steals in one season?

6. Who are the top three players on the Red Sox all-time stolen base list?

7. He holds the career record for most intentional walks. Who is he?

At the Plate—Questions

8. This premier pinch hitter played his final season (1962) in Boston hitting only .143. Name him.

9. Name the first Red Sox player to win a batting title.

10. What category did Ted Williams lead the AL in six straight times?

11. Who was baseball's last .400 hitter?

12. What Red Sox player set a major league record, reaching base an incredible 16 straight times?

13. Who was the first Red Sox opponent to hit three homers in one game in Fenway Park?

14. In 1978 Jim Rice became the first AL player since who to get over 400 total bases?

15. Before Jim Rice did it in 1977, who was the last Red Sox player to total more than 30 homers, 20 doubles and 10 triples in one season?

16. Name two Red Sox players who won at least two batting titles and who have lifetime batting averages below .300.

17. Who was the only Red Sox player to pinch hit for both Ted Williams and Carl Yastrzemski?

18. What pitcher allowed Ted Williams's dramatic last-at-bat home run?

At the Plate—Questions

19. Who was the only Red Sox player to win a home run title between 1949 and 1967?

20. Who was the last Red Sox player to reach the 200-hit plateau before Jim Rice did it in 1977?

21. Only one Red Sox player has led the league in stolen bases more than once. Name him.

22. The lowest average needed to win a batting title was recorded by what Red Sox player?

23. Who was the Red Sox only one-season 50-homer slugger?

24. Who is the only Red Sox 300 career stolen base thief?

25. What Red Sox rookie broke in with four hits as DH in a 1977 game?

26. What Red Sox player led the AL in both runs scored and hits in 1903?

27. Name the Red Sox player who in 1928 tied the major league record of eight total bases in one inning.

28. What was the significance of Ted Williams's sixth (final) batting title?

29. Name the current Red Sox player to be named the 1979 AL MVP.

30. Who is the only man in Red Sox history to hit three triples in one game?

At the Plate—Questions

31. A Yaz three-run, next-to-the-last game homer against Minnesota on September 30, 1967 sent the Sox to the season's final game. Name the Twins hurler victimized.

32. Name the former Red Sox player who remains the all-time doubles champ.

33. Other than Ted Williams (who did it three times) who are the only two players in major league history to walk more than 150 times in one season? Both "wore" Red Sox uniforms at one point.

34. The Red Sox dealt two-time batting champion Pete Runnels to Houston for whom?

35. Why did Red Sox then-rookie slugger Jim Rice miss the '75 Series?

36. Name the Red Sox player who in 1947 hit a "foul ball" triple.

37. What Red Sox player won a 1969 game with a 20th-inning home run?

38. Name the Red Sox base-stealing thief who successfully swiped second immediately after walking in a 1934 game.

39. What Red Sox player had 200-plus hits in each of his first three seasons (also a major league record)?

40. Name the Red Sox player who had a 0 for 44 and eventual 1 for 55 streak?

At the Plate—Questions

41. Who was the Red Sox record-holder for most hits in one season previous to Wade Boggs?

42. The Red Sox clinched the 1946 AL pennant on the only inside-the-park homer of what player's career?

43. How many batting crowns did Ted Williams capture?

44. What did Ted Williams hit in his only World Series appearance?

45. What single-season record do Chick Stahl and Tris Speaker share?

46. Who was the Red Sox' first DH?

47. Name the Red Sox player, traded to the club from Detroit in 1932, who won the batting title the same season.

48. Harvard's all-time batting leader was active with the Sox during the 1986 season. Name him.

49. What Red Sox player scored baseball's "1,000,000th run" while in the NL?

50. What two all-time offensive records for rookies does Ted Williams hold?

51. How many 200-hit seasons did Ted Williams achieve?

52. What future Red Sox player finished second to Yaz for the 1968 AL batting title?

47

At the Plate—Questions

53. How many homers did the Sox hit during their June, '77 ten-game spree?

54. Who did Yaz get his 400th home run off of?

55. Who did Yaz get his 3,000th hit off of?

56. What Red Sox player drove in six runs in one inning in 1945?

57. Name two Red Sox players to hit 30 homers in both leagues.

58. What was Yaz's batting average for the 1967 and 1975 World Series?

59. Who was the last Sox player to switch-hit homers in one game?

60. What pitcher allowed Yaz's first hit?

61. What was Ted Williams's hit total in the historic final day doubleheader against Philadelphia in 1941?

62. What were Carl Yastrzemski's incredible offensive totals for the final two weeks of the 1967 season?

63. After his broken collarbone in spring training, 1954, Ted Williams debuted on May 16 against Detroit with an amazing doubleheader hitting performance. What was it?

64. Three great hitting tears in Red Sox history:
    a) 1938—6 games—17 for 24 (.708)

At the Plate—Questions

    b) 1941—5 games—14 for 20 (.700)
    c) 1974—7 games—17 for 28 (.609)
Name these three players.

65. Who was the first major league player to make 12 consecutive hits?

66. Who was the Red Sox player to total three hits in one inning?

67. Who went 6 for 6 in a 1953 game?

68. Who is the Red Sox record-holder for longest hitting streak?

69. Name the two Red Sox players to be among the select group of those hitting two grand slams in one game?

70. Who established a Red Sox record with four grand slams in one season (1919)?

71. Who did Ted Williams homer against on his "day" at Fenway before returning to the Marines in 1952?

72. What Red Sox player became the first to hit two homers in a game?

73. What Red Sox player hit two homers in the deciding game of the 1915 World Series?

74. Who hit two homers for Boston in the second game of the 1903 (first) World Series?

75. Name the Red Sox player to hit an inside-the-park home run in his first time at bat as a Red Sox?

At the Plate—Questions

76. Who has the longest home run to right field in the "modern" Fenway Park?

77. What Red Sox player was the first to clear Detroit's triple-deck roof?

78. What Red Sox slugger cleared Comiskey Park's left-field roof in 1936?

79. Who broke Clyde Vollmer's record of 13 homers in a month?

80. Who was the first Red Sox player to hit three homers in a game?

81. What Red Sox player slugged 34 homers as a 1950 rookie?

82. What Red Sox player "kicked" a ball over the right-field fence for a 1960 Cleveland homer?

83. What Red Sox player hit pinch homers in two consecutive games?

84. Name the Red Sox player to record two pinch singles in one inning in 1962.

85. Name the two Red Sox players who drove in ten runs in one game.

86. What Red Sox player ended a 1969 1 for 24 slump with a three-homer game against Minnesota?

87. Yaz ended his 0 for 18 1967 slump with an 11th-inning homer off what Yankee moundsman?

88. The Red Sox led the league in triples in

At the Plate—Questions

1972 with 34. Who was the individual leader?

89. Ted Williams boasted two triple crown seasons (1942 and 1947). He narrowly missed two others in 1941 and 1949. Who spoiled those campaigns?

90. What still-active ex-Red Sox player hit a homer in his first at-bat as a starter?

91. Name the Red Sox player who captured the 1960 and 1962 batting titles.

92. During the 1975 Sox pennant-winning season, what player achieved a team-leading, 22-game hitting streak?

93. Who is the only utility player in baseball history to win a batting title?

94. What Detroit Tigers slugger was accused of betting with Ted Williams on the number of homers, RBI's and the batting average the two would compile during the 1946 season?

95. Tommy Harper's 54 stolen bases in 1972 broke what player's 60-year old team record?

96. Name the Red Sox player who captured the league home run title in 1919.

97. Who was the Red Sox's first RBI champion, winning back-to-back titles in 1902 and 1903?

98. Whom did Ted Williams beat out for the

At the Plate—Questions

1958 AL batting title on the season's final day?

99. What Red Sox player was baseball's youngest home run champion?

100. Where did Yaz hit his first home run? Who was the pitcher?

101. Since Tommy Harper's 54 to lead the league in 1973, what is the most steals by a Red Sox player?

102. Name the three Red Sox players to either lead or tie for the league lead in home runs during the 1980s.

103. In 1986 Wade Boggs became the first player since whom to get 200 hits and 100 walks?

104. Who is the Red Sox all-time one season RBI champion?

105. Name the Red Sox player who became the first to hit for the cycle in both leagues.

106. Who was the Kansas City Royals pitcher when Tommy Harper stole home in 1973?

107. Name the Red Sox player who stole five bases in a 1967 doubleheader?

108. Name the Red Sox player who recorded his 500th stolen base while with the club in 1973.

At the Plate—Questions

109. Who set an AL record by being intentionally walked 33 times in one season?

110. The Red Sox hold the AL record for most runs scored in an inning with how many?

111. The American League record for runs scored in a game by both teams (36) was set in 1950 as the Red Sox defeated what club?

112. The Sox set a record for runs scored by one team in 1950 with 29 against what club?

113. Name the Red Sox player who bunted into a triple play against Washington in 1954.

114. Name the Red Sox player to hit for the cycle in 1962 at Kansas City.

115. Name the Red Sox player who established a record by grounding into 32 double plays in 1954.

116. What was the added significance of Carl Yastrzemski's 1965 cycle against Detroit?

117. Carl Yastrzemski's only three-homer game was against what team?

118. What three categories did Fred Lynn lead the AL in during his rookie season?

119. What Red Sox player holds the major league record for doubles in one season?

At the Plate—Questions

120. Name this original New York Met who led the Red Sox in RBI's in 1965?

121. Name the Red Sox slugger to receive a major league record six walks in a single game?

122. Who did Yaz lose the 1970 AL batting title to by .003?

123. Who are the only Red Sox players to collect 200 hits in a season three times?

124. Name the Red Sox all-time great who hit for the cycle in 1940.

125. Name the former Red Sox player who hit .343 as an AL rookie, a record.

126. Who is the only Red Sox player to hit for the cycle twice for Boston?

ANSWERS

1. Dick Stuart

2. Most strikeouts

3. Ken Williams

4. Dom DiMaggio (1950)

5. Tommy Harper (54 in 1973)

6. Harry Hooper (300), Tris Speaker (266) and Carl Yastrzemski (168)

7. Carl Yastrzemski

8. Dave Philley

9. Dale Alexander (.367 in 1932)

10. Walks

11. Ted Williams (.406 in 1941)

12. Ted Williams—four home runs, two singles, nine walks and one hit batsman

At the Plate—Answers

13. The Yankees' Lou Gehrig (June 23, 1927)

14. Joe DiMaggio (1937)

15. Ted Williams

16. Pete Runnels and Carl Yastrzemski

17. Carroll Hardy

18. Baltimore's Jack Fischer—September 28, 1960

19. Tony Conigliaro (32 in 1965)

20. Johnny Pesky (207 in 1947)

21. Bill Werber (46 in 1934 and 29 in 1935)

22. Carl Yastrzemski (.301 in 1968)

23. Jimmie Foxx (1938)

24. Harry Hooper

25. Ted Cox (at Baltimore)

26. Pat Dougherty

27. Bill Regan (two homers)

28. At age 39, he was the oldest player ever to win a title.

29. Don Baylor—while playing for the California Angels

30. Pat Dougherty (September 5, 1903 against Philadelphia)

At the Plate—Answers

31. Jim Merritt

32. Tris Speaker (793)

33. Babe Ruth and Eddie Yost—Red Sox third base coach (1977-1984)

34. Roman Mejias

35. His hand was broken by Detroit's Vern Ruhle.

36. Jake Jones—Fred Sanford, pitching for the St. Louis Browns threw his glove at a ball that rolled foul off the bat of Jones.

37. Joe Lahoud

38. Billy Werber

39. Johnny Pesky

40. Luis Aparicio (1971)—at one point he received a note of condolence from President Nixon.

41. Tris Speaker (222 in 1912)

42. Ted Williams

43. Six—1941, '42, '47, '48, '57 and '58

44. 200—5 for 25

45. Triples (22)—Stahl in 1904 and Speaker in 1913

46. Orlando Cepeda (1973)

At the Plate — Answers

47. Dale Alexander (.367)

48. Mike Stenhouse (.422—1977-79)

49. Bob Watson

50. Walks (107) and RBI's (145)

51. None—his most was 194 in 1949.

52. Danny Cater (.296)

53. 33

54. Mike Morgan of the Oakland A's (July 24, 1979)

55. Yankee Jim Beattie—(September 12, 1979)

56. Tom McBride

57. Dick Stuart and Reggie Smith

58. .352

59. Reggie Smith, who did it four times

60. Ray Herbert of the Kansas City Athletics allowed his first hit on April 11, 1961.

61. Ted went 6 for 8 to finish at .406.

62. 5 HR's, 16 RBI's, 14 runs scored and a .523 average!

63. He went 8 for 9 with two HR's and seven RBI's.

At the Plate—Answers

64. Mike Higgins, Ted Williams and Carlton Fisk

65. Mike Higgins (1938)

66. Gene Stephens (1953)

67. Jim Piersall

68. Dom DiMaggio (34 games)

69. Jim Tabor (1939) and Rudy York (1946)

70. Babe Ruth

71. Detroit's Dizzy Trout

72. Buck Freeman (1901)

73. Harry Hooper

74. Pat Dougherty—the first an inside-the-park

75. John Kennedy

76. Ted Williams—33 rows up off of Detroit's Fred Hutchinson (June 9, 1946)

77. Ted Williams—as a 1939 rookie

78. Jimmie Foxx

79. Jackie Jensen hit 14 in June, 1955.

80. Jim Tabor—at Philadelphia in 1939

At the Plate—Answers

81. Walt Dropo

82. Lou Clinton

83. Chuck Schilling

84. Russ Nixon, against Chicago

85. Norm Zauchin (May 27, 1955) and Rudy York (July 27, 1946)

86. Joe Lahoud

87. Al Downing

88. Carlton Fisk (9)

89. In 1949 George Kell nosed out Ted for the batting crown .3429 to .3427. In 1941 Joe DiMaggio won the RBI title 125-120.

90. Fred Lynn (1974)

91. Pete Runnels

92. Denny Doyle

93. Billy Goodman (.354 in 1950)

94. Dick Wakefield

95. Tris Speaker (52 in 1912)

96. Babe Ruth (29)

97. Buck Freeman

98. Teammate Pete Runnels

At the Plate—Answers

99. Tony Conigliaro, age 22 (1965)

100. Wrigley Field on May 9, 1961 against the Los Angeles Angels—Jerry Casale was on the mound.

101. 30 by Jerry Remy in 1978

102. Tony Armas (43 in 1984), Jim Rice (39 in 1983) and Dwight Evans (22 in 1981)

103. Stan Musial

104. Jimmie Foxx (175 in 1938)

105. Bob Watson

106. Dick Drago

107. Reggie Smith

108. Luis Aparicio

109. Ted Williams

110. 17—against Detroit on June 18, 1953 at Fenway Park

111. The Sox beat the Philadelphia Athletics 22-14 on June 29, 1950 at Shibe Park.

112. The St. Louis Browns on June 8 at Fenway Park

113. Marv Olson

114. Lou Clinton

115. Jackie Jensen

At the Plate—Answers

116. He hit two home runs off Denny McLain, giving him 14 total bases—setting a Sox record for left-handed hitters.

117. The Detroit Tigers (1976)

118. Doubles (47), runs (103) and slugging percentage (.566)

119. Earl Webb with 67 (1931)

120. Felix Mantilla

121. Jimmie Foxx (1938)

122. Alex Johnson

123. Johnny Pesky, Jim Rice and Wade Boggs

124. Joe Cronin

125. Dale Alexander

126. Bobby Doerr (May 17, 1944, at home and May 13, 1947, away)

THE BATTERY QUESTIONS

1. What current Red Sox hurler signed with the club because "Carl Yastrzemski is my favorite ..."?

2. Name the local product (Haverhill, Massachusetts) to catch for the 1967 Red Sox.

3. What record did Red Sox hurler Sammy Stewart establish in his first major league game with Baltimore?

4. What college did Joe Sambito attend?

5. What four players did the Cincinnati Reds trade for then New York Met Tom Seaver?

6. "Oil Can" Boyd's college coach was a former major league pitcher with Houston and St. Louis. Name the hurler.

7. What major league club did Red Sox pitcher Tim Lollar break in with?

The Battery—Questions

8. What current Sox hurler was the losing pitcher in Fenway's longest game?

9. Name the current Red Sox pitcher whose 11 wins as a rookie were the most since John Curtis won 11 in 1972.

10. Bruce Hurst was the first Red Sox player since Bob Stanley to accomplish what in 1980?

11. What Massachusetts high school did Rich Gedman attend?

12. Who did Roger Clemens defeat for the 1983 NCAA Baseball Championship?

13. What Red Sox player was the NCAA player-of-the-year for 1983?

14. In 1953 whom did the Red Sox acquire in exchange from the Chicago White Sox for Vern Stephens?

15. In 1978 the Red Sox received pitcher Dennis Eckersley and catcher Fred Kendall from the Cleveland Indians in exchange for what three players?

16. The Red Sox lost the 1949 pennant to the Yankees on the season's final day. Who was the starter and loser for Boston?

17. In 1966 whom did the Red Sox receive from the Cleveland Indians in exchange for pitcher Dick Radatz?

18. Who was the first Red Sox pitcher to reach the 100 save mark?

The Battery—Questions

19. Who did the Red Sox trade to the Philadelphia Phillies for pitcher Gene Conley in 1960?

20. What Red Sox pitcher has the best career winning percentage against the Yankees—based on at least 20 decisions?

21. Previous to Carlton Fisk who held the Red Sox record for most homers by a catcher?

22. Name the Red Sox catcher unanimously selected as the AL's Rookie of the Year in 1972.

23. Who was the last AL pitcher to get a hit before the DH rule?

24. Who was the former Red Sox pitcher from Michigan St. who averaged more than one strikeout per inning pitched for his career?

25. Name the righty/lefty duo from the 1976 Twins who found themselves together again in the 1980 Red Sox bullpen.

26. Name the only black pitcher to ever win a World Series game for the Red Sox.

27. The 1949 Red Sox—pennant losers by one game—boasted a pair of 20-game winners. Name the duo.

28. Who were the two 20-game winners on the 1946 Red Sox pennant winners?

The Battery—Questions

29. Name the Red Sox pitcher who both won and lost 20 games with the Cleveland Indians.

30. What Red Sox pitcher hit two home runs in support of his no-hitter while in the National League?

31. What Red Sox lefty holds the AL record for shutouts?

32. Who was the ex-Red Sox pitcher to get the loss in Jim Bunning's perfect game?

33. Name the Red Sox pitcher who led the AL in saves in 1946.

34. Name the former Red Sox pitcher to hit four consecutive homers while in the National League.

35. What Red Sox pitcher holds the career record of 39 home runs lifetime?

36. Name the Red Sox pitcher who debuted with a 2-0 shutout at Philadelphia in 1945.

37. What Red Sox pitcher, traded to the Yankees in 1929, went on to average 16 wins per season for the next 13 years?

38. Who was the Red Sox pitcher to beat the Yankees five times in 1953?

39. Name the pitcher who, along with Pumpsie Green and Don Buddin, was involved in a consecutive homer spree (3) against the Yankees.

The Battery—Questions

40. Name the local (Belmont High) pitching star to win 20 games four times after being traded west.

41. Name the Sox pitcher from Medford, Massachusetts who defeated the Yankees 19 times in his career.

42. Who holds the AL record for fewest hits (1) allowed in two consecutive games?

43. Who were the only Red Sox brother battery mates in history?

44. Prior to Roger Clemens, what three Red Sox pitchers have led the league in strikeouts?

45. What Red Sox hurler tossed two one-hitters during the 1976 season?

46. What Red Sox hurler holds the major league record for one-season ERA (1.01, 233 innings)?

47. What Red Sox pitcher dramatically debuted on April 14, 1967?

48. What Red Sox hurler led the AL in ERA four times?

49. Who led the Red Sox in wins in both 1956 and 1957?

50. Who was the last Red Sox pitcher to get a base hit previous to the DH rule?

51. What Red Sox pitcher won two games in one day during August, 1918?

The Battery—Questions

52. Who is the Red Sox all-time winningest left-hander?

53. What Yankee pitcher was the first to ride in the Red Sox bullpen cart?

54. Who were Carlton Fisk's two predecessors behind the plate?

55. What Red Sox pitcher (1926-32) attended Somerville High School?

56. What Red Sox pitcher was quoted as saying he was "in the twilight of a mediocre career"?

57. What Red Sox pitcher held the club single-game strikeout record with 17 prior to Roger Clemens?

58. The AL's first Cy Young Award winner played for the Sox in 1963. Name him.

59. In 1977 the Red Sox dispatched pitcher Ferguson Jenkins to Texas for what player?

60. What Red Sox hurler allowed a record 37 homers in 1964?

61. Name the Red Sox pitcher selected to the 1963 NL and 1969 AL All-Star teams.

62. What early Red Sox hurler went on to coach at Yale?

63. How many 20-win seasons did Babe Ruth have for the Red Sox?

The Battery—Questions

64. Name the Red Sox pitcher to lose a club-record 25 games in a season.

65. Who was the last Sox pitcher to hit a home run before the DH rule?

66. Who was selected the AL's rookie pitcher of the year in 1969?

67. Whose record did Carlton Fisk break for catching the most games in a Sox uniform?

68. What Red Sox pitcher took the loss in the 1964 All Star Game?

69. Who holds the Red Sox record for home runs by a pitcher in one season?

70. Name the Red Sox catcher who holds both the one-season and career home run marks at his position.

71. Who did the Sox give up for pitcher Tom Sturdivant?

72. Who holds the Red Sox record for most saves in one season by a left-hander?

73. Name the Red Sox pitcher who started his career by hurling two straight shutouts.

74. What Yankee pitcher hit three Red Sox hitters in a span of nine pitches in a 1945 game at Fenway?

75. In an infamous Fenway incident, Red Sox catcher Bob Tillman hit the back of

The Battery—Questions

the head of what Sox reliever in his attempt to throw out Al Kaline stealing?

76. Name the Red Sox no-hit pitcher to win his game with a home run.

77. What Red Sox pitcher hit two homers in a game four times?

78. Name the Red Sox reliever who gave up seven homers in an 11-inning span in 1969.

79. Name the Red Sox relief pitcher to also catch.

80. Name the Red Sox record-setting hurler from the 1912 season who was 34-5, struck out 258 batters and won 16 consecutive games during one stretch.

81. Name the Red Sox pitcher who won 13 consecutive games down the stretch for the ill-fated 1949 Red Sox.

82. Who set a record with 70 Red Sox relief appearances in 1960?

83. What Red Sox starter won his last eight decisions in 1967?

84. Name the two Red Sox pitchers to hurl four consecutive shutouts—one in 1968, the other in 1972.

85. What Red Sox pitcher struck out an incredible 478 batters in 414 innings over a three-year span?

The Battery—Questions

86. Name the Red Sox pitcher to hold the Cardinals scoreless for 12 2/3 innings in the 1946 World Series.

87. Who won his first ten decisions as a 1961 rookie?

88. Name two Red Sox pitchers who won both games of a doubleheader.

89. What prompted Gene Conley's flight to Israel in 1962?

90. What two Red Sox pitchers became the first to throw a doubleheader shutout?

91. What Red Sox pitcher from the 1940s was born outside the US?

92. Roger Maris's record-breaking 61st home run came off what Red Sox pitcher?

93. Name four Red Sox starting catchers who were native New Englanders.

94. What Red Sox pitcher made his debut at Fenway Park on July 11, 1914?

95. Name the pitcher who finished his career with the Sox in 1952 and is the only man to pitch to both Babe Ruth and Mickey Mantle.

96. Who led the Red Sox in wins in both 1969 and 1970?

97. Who was the AL's winning percentage leader in 1948?

The Battery—Questions

98. What Red Sox catcher of the 1930s became better-known for his espionage activities?

99. What pitcher did Tom Yawkey offer $1 million for in 1957?

100. Who pitched the Red Sox' first night game no-hitter?

101. What two Sox catchers caught three no-hitters each?

102. What Red Sox pitcher defeated Brooklyn 2-1 on October 9, 1916, in the World Series' longest game?

103. Who was the Red Sox' only left-handed catcher?

104. Name the only two Red Sox pitchers to win 20 games during the 1960s.

105. The Red Sox received pitchers Chesley Church and Jack Ryan along with $12,500 in exchange for what all-time great moundsman?

106. What former Sox hurler allowed Henry Aaron's 700th homer?

107. In 1973 the Red Sox received pitcher Dick Drago from the Kansas City Royals in exchange for what player?

108. Ron Guidry of the Yankees tied the AL record for shutouts by a lefty in 1978 with nine. Whose record did he tie?

The Battery—Questions

109. Name the Red Sox pitcher who won his first 11 decisions in 1973.

110. Who was the lone 20-game winner on the Sox' 1918 world championship team?

111. How many more games did Billy Rohr win after pitching a near no-hitter in his first major league start?

112. What Red Sox starting pitcher from 1959-66 went on to pitch in the 1968 World Series for the Detroit Tigers?

113. Name the youngest and oldest Red Sox no-hit hurlers.

114. On July 14, 1978, two ex-Red Sox pitchers combined to shut out their former manager. Name them.

115. Who is the Red Sox all-time save leader (lefty)?

116. What Red Sox pitcher leads in years of service for the Sox?

117. Name the Red Sox only Cy Young Memorial Award winner.

118. Name the Cleveland Indians outfielder who crashed into Carlton Fisk, ending Fisk's 1974 season.

119. What early Red Sox pitcher was credited with a perfect game that he did not start?

The Battery—Questions

120. The pitcher who allowed Hank Aaron's record-tying 714th home run was briefly with the Sox in 1980. Name the hurler.

121. Name the Red Sox pitcher from the 1970s who won a game against every major league team.

122. What two Red Sox southpaws shut out the Yankees in a critical July, 1975, doubleheader?

123. Name the Red Sox catcher who recorded an eight-assist game on May 12, 1920.

124. Name the Red Sox pitcher who walked ten men and threw 181 pitches in a 1937 game, but won 3-2.

125. Who was the Red Sox reliever who walked an incredible 11 batters in a 4-inning 1943 relief stint?

126. After pitcher Bill Werle threw nine consecutive balls in a 1954 game, Red Sox manager Lou Boudreau replaced his catcher. Name that catcher.

127. The Red Sox combined with the moundsmen of what team to walk 26 batters in one 1961 game?

128. Name the Red Sox catcher whose plate-blocking technique prevented the Yankees from tying the 1971 opener?

129. What Red Sox pitcher debuted with a 10-strikeout win in 1963?

ANSWERS

1. Steve Crawford

2. Mike Ryan

3. He struck out seven consecutive batters —September 1, 1978.

4. Adelphi University

5. Infielder Doug Flynn, pitcher Pat Zachry and outfielders Dan Norman and Steve Henderson—June 15, 1977

6. Scipio Spinks

7. The San Diego Padres

8. Bob Stanley—20 innings against Seattle on September 3 and 4, 1981

9. Al Nipper (11-6, in 1984)

10. He made the jump from Double A to the majors as Stanley had in 1977.

11. St. Peter's (Worcester)

The Battery—Answers

12. Alabama (4-3)

13. Calvin Schiraldi

14. Pitchers Bill Kennedy, Marv Grissom and Skinny Brown

15. Pitcher Mike Paxton, third baseman Ted Cox and catcher Bo Diaz

16. Ellis Kinder

17. Pitchers Lee Stange and Don McMahon

18. Dick Radatz (104)

19. Pitcher Frank Sullivan

20. Babe Ruth (17-5)

21. Bob Tillman, 17 in 1964

22. Carlton Fisk

23. Ken Brett—then with Milwaukee

24. Dick Radatz—745 K's in 693 2/3 innings pitched

25. Bill Campbell and Tom Burgmeier

26. John Wyatt

27. Mel Parnell and Ellis Kinder

28. Tex Hughson and Dave Ferris

29. Luis Tiant

The Battery—Answers

30. Rick Wise

31. Babe Ruth—9 in 1916

32. Tracy Stallard

33. Bob Klinger with 9

34. Ken Brett

35. Lefty Grove

36. Dave Ferris

37. Red Ruffing

38. Mel Parnell

39. Jerry Casale (1959)

40. Wilbur Wood of the Chicago White Sox

41. Bill Monbouquette (1958-65)

42. Howard Ehmke (1923)

43. Wes and Rick Ferrell (1934-37)

44. Jim Lonborg (246 in 1967); Cy Young (159 in 1901); and Tex Hughson (113 in 1942)—tied with Bobo Newson of the Washington Senators

45. Rick Wise—June 14 at Minnesota and June 29 at Baltimore

46. Dutch Leonard (1914)

47. Billy Rohr pitched a one-hitter against the Yankees.

The Battery—Answers

48. Lefty Grove (1935, 1936, 1938 and 1939)

49. Tom Brewer 19-9 (1956) and 16-13 (1957)

50. Luis Tiant (1972)

51. Carl Mays

52. Mel Parnell (123 wins)

53. Luis Arroyo (1960)

54. Bob Montgomery and Duane Josephson

55. Danny MacFayden

56. Frank Sullivan (1953-60)

57. Bill Monbouquette (May 12, 1961)

58. Bob Turley—he won with the Yankees in 1958.

59. Pitcher John Poloni and $20,000

60. Earl Wilson

61. Ray Culp

62. Joe Wood

63. Two—1916 (23-12) and 1917 (23-13)

64. Red Ruffing (1928)

65. Marty Pattin on September 26, 1972

The Battery—Answers

66. Mike Nagy

67. Sammy White (967)

68. Dick Radatz—he gave up a home run to the Phillies' Johnny Callison

69. Wes Ferrell (7 in 1935)

70. Carlton Fisk—26 (1973, 1977) and 162

71. Catcher Pete Daley

72. Tom Burgmeier (24 in 1980)

73. Dave Ferris (1945)

74. Tom Morgan hit Billy Goodman, Ted Lepcio and Milt Bolling.

75. Jim Wyatt (1967)

76. Earl Wilson (2-0 against California on June 26, 1962)

77. Wes Ferrell

78. Fred Wenz

79. Mike Ryba

80. Smokey Joe Wood

81. Ellis Kinder

82. Mike Fornieles

83. Jose Santiago

The Battery—Answers

84. Ray Culp (39 innings) and Luis Tiant (42 1/3 innings)

85. Dick Radatz

86. Joe Dobson

87. Don Schwall

88. Ray Collins (1914) and Carl Mays (1919)

89. A rocky game against the Yankees in which he allowed eight runs

90. Tom Brewer and Bob Porterfield (July 17, 1956)

91. Oscar Judd (London, Ontario, Canada)

92. Tracy Stallard

93. Bill Carrigan (Lewiston, Me.), Birdie Tebbetts (Burlington, Vt.), Carlton Fisk (Bellows Falls, Vt., raised in Charleston, N.H.) and Rich Gedman (Worcester, Mass.)

94. Babe Ruth

95. Al Benton

96. Ray Culp (17 both years)

97. Jack Kramer (18-5)

98. Moe Berg

99. Herb Score (Cleveland Indians)

The Battery—Answers

100. Earl Wilson (June 26, 1962)

101. Lou Criger and Bill Carrigan

102. Babe Ruth (6 hits, 14 innings)

103. Tom Doran (1904-06)

104. Jim Lonborg (22-9 in 1967) and Bill Monbouquette (20-10 in 1963)

105. Cy Young—sent to Cleveland in 1909

106. Ken Brett

107. Pitcher Marty Pattin

108. Babe Ruth (1916)

109. Roger Moret

110. Carl Mays (21-13)

111. One

112. Earl Wilson

113. Joe Wood (21) and Cy Young (37)

114. Fergie Jenkins and Reggie Cleveland (Texas Rangers)

115. Sparky Lyle

116. Ike Delock (12 years—1951-63)

117. Jim Lonborg (1967)

118. Leron Lee

The Battery—Answers

119. Ernie Shore (1917)

120. Jack Billingham, then with the Reds

121. Rick Wise

122. Roger Moret and Bill Lee

123. Wally Schang

124. Buck Newsom

125. Ken Chase

126. Sammy White

127. The Washington Senators

128. Duane Josephson

129. Dave Morehead

PHOTOGRAPHS

1. What food has Wade Boggs become synonymous with?

Photographs—Questions

Jim Rice

2. Where did Sox slugger Jim Rice win his "triple crown"?

Photographs—Questions

3. What is Roger Clemens's real first name? Where was he born?

Photographs—Questions

4. Where did Dennis "Oil Can" Boyd get his nickname?

Photographs—Questions

5. Tom Yawkey donated the first-base stands at what famous park in 1939?

Photographs—Questions

6. Ted Williams always showed disdain for what article of proper male attire?

Photographs—Questions

7. Before Jim Rice, this player was the only one in Red Sox history to put together three consecutive 200-hit seasons. Who is he?

Photographs—Questions

8. When did Yaz capture his first batting title?

Photographs—Questions

9. How many wins did Jim Lonborg have against the Minnesota Twins before the final game of the 1967 season?

Photographs—Questions

10. Name the pictured Sox players with Yaz.

Photographs—Questions

11. This duo formed a memorable Red Sox radio team. Who are they?

Photographs—Questions

12. This Red Sox player made a successful transition from the infield to the outfield. Who is he?

94

Photographs—Questions

13. This Sox slugger found stardom after a controversial trade west. Who is he?

Photographs—Questions

14. Sox coach for nine seasons, this man arrived with the Impossible Dreamers and entertained with his House of David antics. Name this Fenway favorite.

Photographs—Questions

15. The Red Sox acquired this veteran NL slugger for the 1975 stretch run. Name him.

Photographs—Questions

16. This Sox infielder made an emphatic spike following the final out of a Yankee Stadium doubleheader sweep. Who is he?

Photographs—Questions

17. Can you name the members of the 1976 Red Sox' post-pennant coaching staff?

Photographs—Questions

18. Who is this still-active fireman who broke in with the 1977 Sox?

Photographs—Questions

19. One of the most hardnosed players ever to put on a Sox uniform, this player finally asked out of the lineup during the '78 stretch drive because of elbow problems. Name him.

Photographs—Questions

20. The Red Sox pitcher shown leaving the game hailed from Swift Current, Saskatchewan. Who is he?

Photographs—Questions

21. Whom did the fiery Rick Burleson replace as the Red Sox' shortstop in 1974?

Photographs—Questions

22. What two AL teams did Luis Tiant pitch for previous to the Red Sox?

Photographs—Questions

23. In 1977 Carlton Fisk became only the fifth catcher in baseball history to accomplish what feat?

Photographs—Questions

24. Fred Lynn played on three NCAA championship teams under what legendary collegiate mentor?

Photographs—Questions

25. Who is this former Sox catcher and what is his current profession?

Photographs—Questions

26. Name the three Sox players conferring in this tense situation.

Photographs—Questions

27. Name this long-standing building and grounds superintendent for the Red Sox.

Photographs—Questions

28. What years did Joe Cronin manage the Sox?

Photographs—Questions

29. When did this famous interference incident take place?

111

Photographs—Questions

30. What had Carlton Fisk just done?

Photographs—Questions

31. Name this Sox skipper.

113

ANSWERS

1. Chicken

2. At Pawtucket in the International League in 1974: 25 HR's, 93 RBI's and a .337 batting average

3. William; Dayton, Ohio

4. From his capacity to drink beer (oil cans are beer cans)

5. Doubleday Field in Cooperstown, New York

6. Neckties

7. Johnny Pesky

8. 1963, with a .321 average

9. None

10. Frank Malzone and Chuck Schilling

11. Ned Martin and Jim Woods

12. Juan Beniquez

Photographs—Answers

13. Cecil Cooper—traded to Milwaukee

14. Eddie Popowski

15. Deron Johnson

16. Bob Heise

17. Left to right: Don Bryant, John Pesky, Darrell Johnson, Stan Williams, Eddie Popowski and Don Zimmer

18. Don Aase, now with the Orioles

19. Butch Hobson

20. Reggie Cleveland

21. Mario Guerrero

22. Cleveland (1964-69) and Minnesota (1971)

23. He scored (102) and drove in (106) over a hundred runs.

24. Rod Dedeaux (USC)

25. Bob Montgomery, color analyst for Red Sox television broadcasts

26. Catcher Carlton Fisk, pitcher Bill Lee and shortstop Rick Burleson

27. Joe Mooney

28. 1935 to 1947

29. Game 3 of the 1975 World Series

Photographs—Answers

30. Won the sixth game of the 1975 World Series with a 12th-inning home run

31. Darrell Johnson

INFIELD QUESTIONS

1. Who was TV 38's 10th Player Award winner in 1984?

2. What two players finished ahead of Wade Boggs for 1982 AL Rookie of the Year honors?

3. Who was the Red Sox shortstop whom observers thought should have a license plate reading "E-6"?

4. What current Red Sox player was a NL batting champion?

5. Name the only Puerto Rican member of the current Red Sox.

6. What current Red Sox tied Jim Rice's Pawtucket Red Sox total base mark with 249 in 1979?

7. Name the current Red Sox player to attend both USC and Arizona St.

8. The all-time major league assist leader among shortstops finished his career in Boston. Name the player.

Infield—Questions

9. Name the ex-Red Sox third baseman once traded to the New York Mets for Amos Otis.

10. Who is the only first baseman in major league history to make three assists in one inning?

11. The Red Sox received first baseman Bob Watson from the Houston Astros in 1979 in exchange for what two players?

12. Name the Red Sox one-season home run leaders at each infield position.

13. Who spiked the ball at third base after squeezing the final out of the last regularly scheduled game of the 1978 season?

14. What Red Sox first baseman made an unassisted triple play against the Cleveland Indians at Fenway Park on September 14, 1923?

15. Name the former Red Sox first baseman who attended Harvard and coached at Dartmouth.

16. Who played first base both before and after Harry Agganis?

17. In 1958 the Red Sox received infielder Pete Runnels from the Washington Senators in exchange for what two players?

18. In 1946 whom did the Red Sox acquire from the Detroit Tigers in exchange for Eddie Lake?

Infield—Questions

19. What Hall of Fame infielder cost the Red Sox a pennant chance by tripping while rounding third in 1972?

20. One of the most one-sided swaps in Red Sox history occurred prior to the 1972 season when Sparky Lyle was shipped to the New York Yankees. Whom did the Sox receive in return?

21. Name the Sox infielder who set an AL record at second base with only eight errors in 1961.

22. When was the last Red Sox triple play?

23. Whom did the Red Sox acquire in exchange for Bill Lee from the Montreal Expos in 1978?

24. Name the Red Sox infield starter in the 1965 All Star Game.

25. This future Red Sox infielder did not hit into a double play in 570 plate appearances during the 1968 season. Name the player.

26. Name the Red Sox third baseman who set a major league record with ten assists in a 1951 game.

27. Who played shortstop on the Red Sox world championship teams in 1915, 1916 and 1918?

28. Who was the Red Sox's Opening Day second baseman in 1967?

Infield—Questions

29. Name the Red Sox infielder knocked unconscious by Nolan Ryan in 1974.

30. Name the Red Sox second baseman to hit two homers in one inning in 1928.

31. Name the Sox "ironman" to play in a club record 832 games from June, 1916 to October, 1921.

32. Who became the Red Sox "player to be named later" in the Denny Doyle deal with California (1975)?

33. In 1966 whom did the Red Sox receive from Houston in exchange for infielder Felix Mantilla?

34. What major league record did shortstop Mario Guerrero tie on June 2, 1973?

35. Carl Yastrzemski was signed out of Notre Dame in 1958 playing what position?

36. What Red Sox infielder established a record with 77 consecutive errorless games at third base in 1971?

37. What Red Sox shortstop set a record by committing three errors in two consecutive games?

38. What position was Carl Yastrzemski pressed into service at in 1973?

39. Name the Red Sox first baseman who accepted 1,651 of 1,652 chances in 1921.

Infield—Questions

40. Who preceded Butch Hobson at third base for the Red Sox?

41. What Red Sox player holds the AL record for most home runs by a shortstop in one season?

42. What Red Sox standout inauspiciously debuted with a three error performance on May 4, 1974?

43. Whom did the Red Sox receive in exchange for George Scott in 1979?

44. In 1954 the Red Sox acquired third baseman Grady Hatton and $100,000 from the Detroit Tigers for what player?

45. Who hit the first home run at Fenway Park?

46. What former Red Sox infielder was quoted as saying the Red Sox were "twenty-five players needing twenty-five taxis"?

47. Who was the Red Sox first Rookie of the Year?

48. Name the Red Sox third baseman (1952-54) who, when with the Orioles, lost his job to Brooks Robinson.

49. Who replaced Eddie Bressoud as the Red Sox shortstop during the 1965 campaign?

50. Who did Eddie Bressoud succeed as the Red Sox shortstop in 1962?

Infield—Questions

51. What former Red Sox infielder did Oakland A's owner Charlie Finley try to "fire" during the 1973 World Series?

52. Name the former Red Sox infielder acquired from Detroit, who once with the Tigers struck out and walked 100 times in the same season.

53. Who did Johnny Pesky twice swap positions with?

54. Name the four post-WWII batting champions to win their titles elsewhere—and then play for the Red Sox. All are infielders.

55. What two players preceded George Scott as the Red Sox regular first baseman?

56. Whom did the Red Sox send to the Chicago White Sox in 1970 in exchange for shortstop Luis Aparicio?

57. What position did Jimmy Piersall play upon coming to the Red Sox in 1950?

58. What Red Sox first baseman set a major league record with 161 assists in one season?

59. What Red Sox third baseman (a converted outfielder) was knocked out of action by a Joe DiMaggio smash in 1946?

60. Who preceded Doug Griffin as the Red Sox second baseman?

Infield—Questions

61. Who preceded Frank Malzone as the Red Sox third baseman?

62. Who followed Frank Malzone as the Red Sox regular third baseman?

63. The Red Sox traded utility infielder Dalton Jones to the Detroit Tigers for whom?

64. Who was the mainstay at shortstop for the Red Sox between 1908 and 1913?

65. Name the first basemen the Red Sox and the Milwaukee Braves swapped in 1960.

66. In 1975 what trade did pitcher Jim Willoughby complete by signing?

67. Name the Red Sox infielder who is credited with three successful hidden ball plays.

68. In 1964 whom did the Red Sox send to the Philadelphia Phillies for pitcher Dennis Bennett?

69. Former Red Sox infielder and current Boston College baseball coach Eddie Pellagrini accomplished what feat in his first major league at bat?

70. Name the light-hitting Kansas City Royals infielder who smashed three homers in a June, 1980 game.

ANSWERS

1. Marty Barrett

2. Cal Ripken and Kent Hrbek

3. Don Buddin

4. Bill Buckner (.324 in 1980 while with the Cubs)

5. Ed Romero

6. Dave Stapleton

7. Bill Buckner

8. Luis Aparicio (1971-73)

9. Joe Foy—pitcher Bob Johnson was also sent to the Royals in the deal.

10. Dick Stuart

11. Pitchers Pete Ladd and Bobby Sprowl

12. 1b—Jimmy Foxx 50 (1938); 2b—Bobby Doerr 27 (1948 and 1950); ss—Rico

Infield—Answers

Petrocelli 40 (1969); and 3b—Butch Hobson 30 (1977)

13. Jack Brohamer

14. George Burns—he caught Frank Brower's line drive going to his right with a hit-and-run play on, tagged Rube Lutzke and beat Riggs Stephenson to second base.

15. Tony Lupien

16. Dick Gernert

17. First baseman Norm Zauchin and outfielder Albie Pearson

18. First baseman Rudy York

19. Luis Aparicio—against Detroit

20. First baseman Danny Cater and shortstop Mario Guerrero

21. Chuck Schilling

22. July 28, 1979 at Texas—the Sox tied a major league record with three in 1979.

23. Utility infielder Stan Papi

24. Felix Mantilla

25. Dick McAuliffe, then playing for the Detroit Tigers

26. Vern Stephens

27. Everett Scott

Infield—Answers

28. Reggie Smith

29. Doug Griffin

30. Bill Regan—the second an inside-the-park

31. Everett Scott, shortstop

32. Pitcher Chuck Ross

33. Future Sox manager Eddie Kasko

34. He figured in 5 double plays.

35. Shortstop

36. Rico Petrocelli

37. Juan Beniquez (1972)

38. Third base

39. Stuffy McInnis (1918-21)

40. Rico Petrocelli

41. Rico Petrocelli, 40 (1969)

42. Shortstop Rick Burleson

43. Tom Poquette from the Kansas City Royals

44. Third baseman George Kell

45. Hugh Bradley—over the left-field wall, the only homer that season (1912) by the Red Sox first baseman

Infield—Answers

46. Frank Duffy

47. First baseman Walt Dropo (1950)

48. George Kell

49. Rico Petrocelli

50. Don Buddin

51. Mike Andrews

52. Dick McAuliffe (1967)

53. Vern Stephens (ss-3b)

54. Mickey Vernon (1b), Bobby Avila (2b), George Kell (3b) and Lou Boudreau (ss)

55. Lee Thomas and Tony Horton (1965)

56. Infielders Mike Andrews and Luis Alvarado

57. Shortstop

58. Bill Buckner (1983)

59. Leon Culbertson

60. Mike Andrews

61. Billy Klaus

62. Joe Foy

63. Infielder Tom Matchik

64. Heinie Wagner

Infield—Answers

65. Ron Jackson to Milwaukee for Ray Boone

66. Shortstop Mario Guerrero's sale to the St. Louis Cardinals

67. Johnny Pesky

68. First baseman Dick Stuart

69. He homered on April 22, 1946 against Washington.

70. Fred Patek

OUTFIELD QUESTIONS

1. The Red Sox had three players who shared right field during the 1946 season. Name the trio.

2. What current Red Sox outfielder has an uncle who pitched for the Chicago White Sox and Cincinnati Reds?

3. Who holds the Red Sox record with 16 total bases in one game?

4. What team did Tony Armas break in with?

5. In 1978 Jim Rice became only the fifth player in AL history to lead the league in what two categories in the same year?

6. Name the former Red Sox outfielder to win the 1969 Big Ten batting championship.

7. Dwight Evans was the 1972 International league MVP while playing for what club?

Outfield—Questions

8. Name the Red Sox one-season home run record-holders at each outfield position.

9. Who did the Red Sox receive from Detroit in exchange for outfielder Ben Oglivie?

10. In 1958 the Red Sox received first baseman Vic Wertz and outfielder Gary Geiger from the Cleveland Indians in exchange for whom?

11. In 1967 whom did the Red Sox acquire from the Chicago Cubs in exchange for outfielder Bill Schleisinger and cash?

12. Whom did Ted Williams replace as the Sox' regular leftfielder?

13. In 1976 the Red Sox traded outfielder Bernie Carbo to Milwaukee for what two players?

14. In 1974 whom did the Red Sox receive in exchange for outfielder Tommy Harper from the California Angels?

15. In 1932 the Red Sox received first baseman Dale Alexander and outfielder Roy Johnson from the Detroit Tigers in exchange for whom?

16. Name the Red Sox outfielder who is acknowledged as the last man to throw out an opposing batter on a clean base hit.

17. Name the Minnesota Twins outfielder who was cut down by Carl Yastrzemski

Outfield—Questions

trying to stretch a single on the final day of the 1967 season.

18. How did Jimmy Piersall injure his arm in 1954?

19. What New York Yankee did Yaz rob with a remarkable catch in Billy Rohr's debut no-hit bid?

20. What three fielders recorded brief pitching stints during Joe Cronin's tenure as Red Sox manager?

21. Who was the Red Sox outfielder who reputedly heaved a ball from home plate over the old center-field wall at a Fenway throwing contest?

22. Who set the AL record for most putouts in a season by an outfielder?

23. Who was the Red Sox centerfielder before Dom DiMaggio?

24. Name the still-active outfielder who broke in as an error-prone shortstop for the 1972 Red Sox.

25. Whom did Ted Williams replace as the Sox' regular left-fielder?

26. During the period 1910-17, what was Fenway's left-field embankment known as?

27. In 1950 whom did the Red Sox receive in exchange for infielder Merrill Combs

Outfield—Questions

and outfielder Tom O'Brien from the Washington Senators?

28. Name the only two players in baseball history to pitch and play the outfield in different World Series?

29. On August 24, 1940, Ted Williams made his infamous two-inning pitching appearance against Detroit. Who replaced Ted in left field?

30. Who used a white glove while playing the outfield for Boston?

31. What Red Sox outfielder (1936-40) used a flat glove with the palm cut out?

32. How high is the "Green Monster"?

33. What was unusual about Dom DiMaggio's positioning in center field?

34. In 1962 the Red Sox sent infielder Pete Runnels to the Houston Colt 45's in exchange for whom?

35. What two Red Sox brothers and outfielders hit 36 and 18 home runs in the same season?

36. Twice the Red Sox have boasted .300 hitting outfields: 1938 and 1950. Name each trio.

37. Who replaced an injured Ted Williams in left field in 1950?

Outfield—Questions

38. What Red Sox outfielder (1960-62) played for the San Francisco 49ers in 1955?

39. What Boston rightfielder was the first to use sunglasses?

ANSWERS

1. Tom McBride, George Metkovich and Wally Moses

2. Dave Henderson—uncle Joe Henderson

3. Fred Lynn—June 18, 1975 against Detroit

4. The Pittsburgh Pirates

5. Hits (213) and homers (46)

6. Rick Miller—while at Michigan St.

7. Louisville, Kentucky

8. Rf—Jackie Jensen 35 (1958); cf—Fred Lynn 39 (1979); and lf—Carl Yastrzemski 44 (1967)

9. Infielder Dick McAuliffe

10. Outfielder Jim Piersall

11. Pitcher Ray Culp

Outfield—Answers

12. Ben Chapman

13. Pitcher Tom Murphy and outfielder Bobby Darwin

14. Infielder Bob Heise

15. Outfielder Earl Webb

16. Lou Finney, who threw out Cleveland catcher Gene Desautels in 1941

17. Bob Allison

18. He was in a throwing contest with Willie Mays.

19. Tom Tresh

20. Doc Cramer, Ted Williams and Jimmie Foxx

21. Smead Jolley

22. Dom DiMaggio (503 in 1948)

23. Doc Cramer

24. Juan Beniquez

25. Ben Chapman (1937-38)

26. Duffy's Cliff

27. Outfielder Clyde Vollmer

28. Babe Ruth and Joe Wood

29. Pitcher Jim Bagby

Outfield—Answers

30. Babe Ruth

31. Doc Cramer

32. 37 feet

33. He would angle himself right or left depending on the batter.

34. Outfielder Roman Mejias

35. Tony and Billy Conigliaro

36. 1938—Joe Vosmik (.324), Doc Cramer (.301) and Ben Chapman (.340); 1950—Ted Williams (.317), Dom DiMaggio (.328) and Al Zarilla (.325)

37. Billy Goodman

38. Carroll Hardy

39. Harry Hooper

MANAGERS AND COACHES QUESTIONS

1. Who was the Red Sox' first manager?

2. Who managed the Red Sox to their last world championship?

3. What four major league clubs did John McNamara manage previous to the Red Sox?

4. Red Sox coach Rene Lachemann managed what two major league teams?

5. Name the Red Sox coach who was a three-sport all-Scholastic choice.

6. Name the Red Sox pitching coach once traded to the Yankees by the Dodgers for Moose Skowron.

7. What was Dick Williams's guarantee upon his arrival as Red Sox manager in 1967?

8. Where did Red Sox co-owner Haywood Sullivan play college football and baseball?

Managers and Coaches—Questions

9. In 1962 future Red Sox manager Dick Williams was acquired by the Red Sox from the Houston Colts in exchange for whom?

10. What Red Sox manager said: "I'm the only chief, all the rest are Indians"?

11. Name the Red Sox skipper to be named Manager of the Year in 1955.

12. Who was the major league Executive of the Year in 1967?

13. What current major league manager managed Carl Yastrzemski in 1960 while with the Minneapolis Millers?

14. The losing pitcher in Don Larsen's 1956 World Series perfect game would later become a Sox pitching coach. Name him.

15. Name the Sox player and later coach to join the elite 30/30 club—homers and stolen bases—before coming to Boston.

16. Who succeeded Joe Cronin as Red Sox manager?

17. Only one Red Sox manager has managed over 2,000 games. Name the skipper.

18. Since the inception of numbers, who was the only Red Sox player, manager or coach not to wear one?

Managers and Coaches—Questions

19. Name the Red Sox pitcher, later coach, who tied a major league record with four strikeouts in an inning?

20. What line of work was ill-fated Red Sox owner (1917-23) Harry Frazee in?

21. Who managed the Red Sox prior to Darrell Johnson?

22. What two brothers managed the Red Sox?

23. What Red Sox manager let a dozen players go home the last day of the season?

24. Name the Red Sox manager/outfielder who died drinking poison during a 1907 barnstorming tour.

25. Name the Red Sox player/manager who set a record with five pinch homers?

26. What was the only AL team former Sox manager Don Zimmer played for?

27. Name the Chicago White Sox manager who intentionally walked Carl Yastrzemski three consecutive times in a 1968 game.

28. Name the Detroit Tiger who, with first base open, was pitched to by manager Eddie Kasko, only to single and give the Tigers the 1972 AL East crown.

29. Name the Red Sox manager who punched a young Babe Ruth.

Managers and Coaches—Questions

30. Who did Red Sox manager Don Zimmer describe as having "icewater in his veins" before an important late season Yankee game in 1978?

ANSWERS

1. Jimmy Collins (1901-07)

2. Edward G. Barrow

3. The Oakland A's, the San Diego Padres, the Cincinnati Reds and the California Angels

4. Milwaukee and Seattle

5. Walt Hriniak—Natick High

6. Stan Williams

7. "We'll win more than we lose."

8. The University of Florida

9. Outfielder Carroll Hardy

10. Dick Williams, upon relieving Carl Yastrzemski of his captaincy at the beginning of the 1967 season

11. Mike Higgins (the team finished fourth.)

Managers and Coaches—Answers

12. Dick O'Connell

13. Gene Mauch

14. Sal Maglie

15. Tommy Harper—with the Milwaukee Brewers in 1970

16. Joe McCarthy (1948)

17. Joe Cronin (2,007)

18. Joe McCarthy—manager from 1948 to 1950

19. Lee Stange—pitching for Cleveland (1964)

20. Theatrical production

21. Eddie Kasko

22. Charles Stahl (1906) and Garland Stahl (1912-13)

23. Billy Jurges (1959)—the Red Sox beat the Senators 6-2.

24. Chick Stahl

25. Joe Cronin

26. The Washington Senators

27. Eddie Stanky

28. Al Kaline

Managers and Coaches—Answers

29. Bill Carrigan

30. Bobby Sprowl—his ill-fated choice as a starter

MISCELLANEOUS QUESTIONS

1. What Red Sox player attained MVP status at the 1970 All Star Game?

2. What college did Tom Seaver pitch for?

3. What Red Sox player's career was ended a result of a fractured ankle suffered at Yankee Stadium in early 1945?

4. What opposing pitcher's "major league" wild pitch hit the top of the screen at Fenway Park on April 16, 1978?

5. What was Cy Young's real middle name and what was it thought to be for years?

6. What "experiment" did the Cleveland Indians perform at Fenway Park on July 14, 1946?

7. Name the future Red Sox pitcher who retrieved Hank Aaron's 715th record-setting home run in 1973.

8. In 1951 Ted Williams was the final out in what opposing pitcher's second no-hitter of the season?

Miscellaneous—Questions

9. Name the New York Yankee who broke up Bob Ojeda's no-hit bid in the 9th inning in September, 1981.

10. Who made an unassisted triple play against the Red Sox?

11. Name the Red Sox third baseman who made the AL all-rookie team in 1980.

12. Who was the Indians starter who defeated the Yankees' "Catfish" Hunter on the 1978 season's final day to force the AL East playoff?

13. What is Sox shortstop Spike Owen's real name?

14. Who are the three members of the Red Sox to play on the 1983 NCAA Baseball Champions?

15. Who was the "Moosup Mauler"?

16. Who was the Narragansett lady on Red Sox telecasts in the 1950s?

17. What former Red Sox player is the only man to be a baseball MVP and a football all-American?

18. What defensive record did the Red Sox tie in a 1952 game at Yankee Stadium?

19. Name the Philadelphia pitcher whom, on Patriots' Day, 1948, Ted Williams hit on the leg the pitcher wounded in WWII.

Miscellaneous—Questions

20. Who was the youngest player to appear in a game for the Red Sox?

21. Who was nicknamed "Indian"?

22. What was Roger Kraven's nickname?

23. Name a Mexican-born Red Sox pitcher.

24. Name four Puerto Rican-born Red Sox pitchers.

25. Name three Cuban-born Red Sox pitchers.

26. Whom did pitcher Carl Mays (1915-1919) kill with an errant beanball?

27. Who described his homers as "taters"?

28. Other than Ted Williams, what Red Sox player wore shinguards at the plate to protect against foul tips?

29. Who preceded Jim Britt as the "voice of the Red Sox"?

30. Whose nickname was "Moe"?

31. Whose nickname was "Ellie"?

32. What were Vernon Stephen's two nicknames?

33. What was William Dineen's nickname?

34. When was the last triple play made against the Red Sox?

Miscellaneous—Questions

35. What is the deepest point in Fenway Park?

36. How high is the screen atop Fenway's "Green Monster"?

37. What is the distance down Fenway's left-field line?

38. What is the short distance directly down Fenway's right-field line?

39. Who was the Red Sox radio voice in the early 50s?

40. Who preceded Art Gleason as Curt Gowdy's broadcast partner?

41. What was Rip Repulski's real name?

42. Yaz made two minor league stops before Fenway. Name the cities.

43. What 1964 Red Sox player graduated from Boston English High School?

44. Where did the Conigliaro brothers hail from?

45. Who did Johnny Pesky replace when he moved to the broadcast booth?

46. What was Sonny Siebert's real first name?

47. What was Doug Griffin's nickname?

48. Who took over Red Sox TV broadcasts in 1974?

Miscellaneous—Questions

49. Who became Ken Coleman's new broadcast partner in 1980?

50. What was the name of the song Tony Conigliaro recorded?

51. What former Red Sox player is Carlton Fisk's brother-in-law?

52. Name the Red Sox pitcher born in Holland.

53. What was the name of the Ken Harrelson-inspired song heard in 1968?

54. Who were the two Red Sox pitchers hit in the face by Hank Greenberg line drives?

55. What was unusual about the Red Sox-Indians games of July 20-21, 1954?

56. What were the characteristics of the Boudreau-shift employed to stop Ted Williams?

57. Name the Red Sox player who tragically died of a pulmonary embolism in 1955.

58. How did Jim Lonborg get hurt in the winter after his Cy Young season?

59. What Red Sox slugger feared air travel?

60. What was "buried" in the Red Sox bullpen during the 1955 season?

61. What Red Sox player bought an accordian to break out of a 1936 slump?

Miscellaneous—Questions

62. Name the California Angels pitcher who struck out 19 Red Sox in a 15-inning game at Anaheim.

63. What was the incredible weather characteristic of Opening Day in 1973?

64. Whose nickname was "Satch"?

65. Whose nickname was "Zeke"?

66. Who was "The Cat"?

67. Three father-son combinations have played for the Red Sox during their history. Name them.

68. What was John Kennedy's nickname?

69. What was Michael Higgins's nickname?

70. What was the Red Sox' only grandfather/grandson combination?

71. What is John Freeman's nickname?

72. From what college did Moe Berg graduate?

73. Where did Dave Ferris play collegiate ball?

74. Who was the Red Sox half of a father-son World Series duo?

75. What was William Carrigan's nickname?

76. What was James Lonborg's nickname?

Miscellaneous—Questions

77. What was Carl Yastrzemski's nickname when he joined the Red Sox in 1961?

78. Whose nickname was "Sonny"?

79. Whose nickname was "Mugsy"?

80. Where did the Red Sox train in 1945?

81. Who was nicknamed "Sparky"?

82. Who were the "buffalo heads"?

83. What member of the 1903 AL Champs hailed from Vermont?

84. Who was nicknamed "Baby Bull" or "Cha Cha"?

85. What was Carl Mays's nickname?

86. Before being officially designated as the Red Sox in 1907, what color were their socks?

87. What ex-Red Sox player replaced Lou Gehrig at first base at the end of Gehrig's 2,130th consecutive game?

88. What was John Collins's nickname?

89. Who were nicknamed "Hoot" and "Scoot"?

90. Name the three products that sponsored the 1967 Red Sox.

91. Who was nicknamed "Candy"?

92. What was Elijah Green's nickname?

Miscellaneous—Questions

93. Ted Williams served in what branch of the service in both World War II and Korea?

94. What charitable organization did Ted Williams's mother work for?

95. The ever-controversial Bill Lee referred to what opponent as "Brownshirts"?

96. Why was Ted Williams once fined $5,000?

97. What year did Ted Williams cut his own salary the full allowable 28 percent?

98. Name three nicknames of Red Sox great Ted Williams.

99. What team originally signed Tom Seaver?

100. Whom did Ted Williams give his entire 1946 World Series check to?

101. What was Ted Williams's incredible vision recorded at?

102. What has always been Ted Williams's acknowledged favorite hobby?

103. What was Lefty Grove's real name?

104. Name the Red Sox pitcher who fell from a horse during spring training in 1960.

105. What Red Sox pitcher fell from a circus elephant?

Miscellaneous—Questions

106. What was the name of Bernie Carbo's stuffed gorilla good-luck charm?

107. Name two Dick Stuart nicknames.

108. Name the Red Sox outfielder who, thinking he had tripled in the winning run in a 1961 game, headed for the dugout, only to be tagged out.

109. Ted Williams's famous bat-throwing tantrum occurred on September 21, 1958. Who was the spectator he hit?

110. What New York Yankee's botched squeeze bunt attempt resulted in the Carlton Fisk-Thurman Munson collision and brawl in 1973?

111. Name the New York Yankees third baseman who committed four errors against the Red Sox in a 1972 game.

112. What was the name for the group of early Red Sox home-game followers?

113. What was the nickname of 1975 Red Sox rookies Jim Rice and Fred Lynn?

114. What was "Sam" Mele's real first name?

115. What is Butch Hobson's real name?

116. Who did the Red Sox receive in exchange for Johnny Pesky?

117. Where did ex-Red Sox third baseman Butch Hobson play college football?

Miscellaneous—Questions

118. Name the Red Sox pitcher who played in the same Kansas backfield as Gayle Sayers.

119. What longevity record does Carl Yastrzemski hold?

120. One of only three men to play in a Rose Bowl and a World Series played for the Red Sox. Name the player.

121. What was James Vernon's real name?

122. In what game did Ted Williams break his arm?

123. Whose nickname was "Old Folks"?

124. Whose nickname was "Duffy"?

125. What was Dominic DiMaggio's nickname?

126. What ex-Red Sox player's father was MVP of the 1953 Orange Bowl?

127. What is written in morse code on the scoreboard in Fenway Park?

128. What was George Tebbetts's nickname?

129. What was Dave Ferris's nickname?

130. What was Richard Schofield's nickname?

131. What is Rick Burleson's nickname?

ANSWERS

1. Carl Yastrzemski—going 4 for 4

2. Southern California

3. Joe Cronin

4. Len Barker of the Texas Rangers

5. True, not Tecumseh

6. The "Ted Williams shift"—developed by Indians manager Lou Boudreau

7. Tom House

8. Allie Reynolds (New York Yankees)

9. Rick Cerone

10. Cleveland shortstop Neal Ball (July 19, 1909)

11. Glenn Hoffman

12. Rick Waits

Miscellaneous—Answers

13. Spike—his mother's maiden name was Spikes.

14. The three Texas Longhorns are Roger Clemens, Calvin Schiraldi and Spike Owen.

15. Walt Dropo

16. Irehne Hennessey

17. Jackie Jensen—MVP in 1958 and all-American at the University of California

18. They totaled 10 assists in an inning.

19. Lou Brissie

20. Jim Pagliaroni (17 years old)

21. Bob Johnson

22. "Doc"

23. Vicente Romo

24. Roger Moret, Juan Pizarro, Jose Santiago and Ramon Hernandez

25. Luis Tiant, Mike Fornieles and Diego Segui

26. Ray Chapman

27. George Scott

28. Vic Wertz

29. Fred Hoey

Miscellaneous—Answers

30. Morris Berg

31. Elston Howard

32. "Buster" and "Junior"

33. Big Bill

34. September 4, 1965 at New York

35. Center field—420 feet

36. 23 feet 7 inches

37. 315 feet

38. 302 feet

39. Curt Gowdy

40. Bob Murphy

41. Eldon

42. Raleigh, North Carolina (1959) and Minneapolis, Minnesota (1960)

43. Bobby Guindon

44. Swampscott, Massachusetts

45. Mel Parnell

46. Wilfred

47. Dude

48. Dick Stockton and Ken Harrelson

Miscellaneous—Answers

49. Jon Miller

50. "Playing the Field"

51. Rick Miller

52. Win Remmerswaal

53. "Don't Walk the Hawk" by Judy Harbison of the Val Perry Trio

54. Fritz Ostermueller (1935) and Jim Wilson (1945)

55. The two clubs played 16 and then 8 innings, both ending in ties.

56. Everyone on the right side, the third baseman behind second and the left fielder playing a deep shortstop.

57. Boston University's Harry Agganis—he was 25 years old.

58. Skiing

59. Jackie Jensen

60. A plastic black cat

61. Oscar Melillo

62. Nolan Ryan

63. Winds gusted to 45 knots as at least six routine flys dropped in. The Sox beat New York 15-5.

64. Catcher Tom Satriano

Miscellaneous—Answers

65. Outfielder Al Zarilla

66. Felix Mantilla

67. Ed Connolly (1929-32) and Ed Connolly, Jr. (1964); Smokey Joe Wood (1908-15) and Joe Wood, Jr., (1944); and Haywood Sullivan (1955, 1957, 1959-60) and Marc Sullivan (1982, 1984-   )

68. Super Sub

69. Pinky

70. John Collins (1921-25) and Robert Gallagher (1972)

71. Buck

72. Princeton

73. Mississippi State

74. Jim Bagby, Jr. (1946)

75. Rough

76. Gentleman Jim

77. Yeasty

78. Pitcher Wilfred Siebert

79. Robert "Denny" Doyle and Gary Allenson

80. Pleasantville, New Jersey

Miscellaneous—Answers

81. Albert Lyle

82. A Red Sox clique of nonconformists in the late 70s, led by Bill Lee

83. Larry Gardner

84. Orlando Cepeda

85. Sub

86. Black

87. Babe Dahlgren

88. Shano

89. Red Sox keystone combo Rick Burleson and Jerry Remy

90. Narragansett Beer, White Owl Cigars and Atlantic Gas

91. George LaChance

92. Pumpsie

93. The Marine Corps, as a pilot

94. The Salvation Army

95. Billy Martin's Yankees

96. He was fined for spitting at fans.

97. His final season, 1960, after injuries resulted in his batting only .254 in 1959.

98. "Splendid Splinter," "The Kid" and "Teddy Ballgame"

Miscellaneous—Answers

99. The Atlanta Braves (1966)—but it was voided by Commissioner William Eckert.

100. Clubhouse man Johnny Orlando

101. 20-10—a 1 in 100,000 probability

102. Fishing

103. Robert Moses Grove

104. Bill Monbouquette

105. Willard Nixon—at Sarasota in 1956

106. Mighty Joe Young

107. "Stonefingers" and "Dr. Strangeglove"

108. Gary Geiger

109. Joe Cronin's housekeeper

110. Gene Michael

111. Rich McKinney—the Sox won 11-7 as the miscues led to nine runs.

112. The Royal Rooters

113. The Goldust Twins

114. Sabath

115. Clell Lavern

116. George Kell

Miscellaneous—Answers

117. Alabama

118. Quarterback Steve Renko

119. Most consecutive years playing in more than 100 games

120. Jackie Jensen

121. Mickey Vernon

122. The All Star Game of 1950

123. Ellis Kinder

124. George Lewis

125. Little Professor

126. Butch Hobson

127. "Tom and Jean"

128. Birdie

129. Boo

130. Ducky

131. Rooster